Table of Contents

Introduction

Many couples ask if sex during pregnancy is safe, especially during the first and third trimesters, and they often worry about harming the baby. But if you have a healthy pregnancy, it's perfectly safe to have sex right up until your waters break. This is true even if you're having more than one baby.

If you're in the right mood, having satisfying sex is good for your relationship and your sense of wellbeing, both now and after your baby has arrived.

Don't feel pressured though. Many women find that their sex drive changes during pregnancy. This can happen because of changing emotions, pregnancy side-effects such as nausea, or simply being really tired – sometimes you might find yourself yearning more for a good night's sleep.

The key is to keep communicating with your partner, and find a balanced way to stay close and feel happy as a couple. Talk to your partner if your sex drive is low to help them understand how you're feeling.

Will sex harm my baby?

You won't hurt your baby by having sex, even with your partner on top. And your little one won't know what you're doing, either. The amniotic sac and the strong muscles of your womb (uterus) will protect your baby, while the thick mucus plug that seals your cervix helps guard against infection.

Other types of sex are generally safe during pregnancy too – though you may need to take some special precautions. Find out more about oral sex, anal sex and using sex toys when you're pregnant.

If you have an orgasm in late pregnancy, you might feel some mild contractions in your womb (known as Braxton Hicks contractions). This is common, especially towards the end of your third trimester. They should pass if you rest for a few minutes. If the contractions continue, or if you are leaking fluid or bleeding after sex, call your midwife or see a doctor to be on the safe side.

Are there times when I shouldn't have sex?

Your midwife or GP may advise you not to have sex if:

- you've experienced bleeding during your pregnancy
- you have an increased risk of miscarriage
- you have a history of cervical weakness or giving birth prematurely
- your placenta is low-lying (placenta praevia)
- your waters have broken

You may also be advised to avoid sex if your partner has an active sexually transmitted infection (STI). If your partner has an STI, or if you think he might, talk to your GP or midwife for specific advice on managing this.

You should also use a condom to protect against STIs if you or your partner are having sex with other people. If you have sex with a new partner while you're pregnant, have an honest conversation about possible STIs and use a condom.

Will sex feel as good during pregnancy?

It depends. It's better for some women, and not as good for others.

Increased blood flow to your pelvic area during pregnancy can heighten sexual sensation – or feel uncomfortable. Some women say they can't get turned on or reach orgasm as easily while they're carrying a baby.

If you find your usual positions uncomfortable, there are other ways to enjoy sex. During pregnancy many couples get pleasure from foreplay, oral sex, sex toys or masturbation. Think of it as a chance to spice up your sex life and try something creative.

I've gone off sex since I got pregnant. Is this normal?

Yes! The big changes in your body and your life are bound to alter your sex life. Some women are just too tired or feel too nauseous to have sex, especially in the first trimester.

Mood changes, backache and sore breasts are some of the other reasons for less interest in sex. Hormonal changes can also cause a loss of libido.

Not surprisingly, your state of mind is important, too. If you feel positive about your pregnancy and the changes to your body, you're likely to feel more sexual. But if you're not particularly happy about the pregnancy, or if you feel insecure, this can put you off sex. It's also a time when you might feel like your identity as a sexual woman doesn't match your role or feelings as a mother.

Even if you enjoyed sex during the first part of your pregnancy, your sex drive can start dropping off as the birth gets closer. This is a common experience for many couples.

Ultimately, everyone's different, and couples who are expecting don't all have the same feelings about sex. What's normal for someone else won't necessarily be the same for you.

Will my partner's sex drive change now that I'm pregnant?

It might. Some men feel less interested in sex, especially in the third trimester.

This doesn't mean that your partner doesn't find you attractive any more – far from it. Many men say they want sex with their partner as much as ever, and they're happy with the relationship during pregnancy.

When it does happen, the reasons for a dad-to-be's lower desire might include:

- fears that sex can hurt the baby
- worries about your health and the health of your baby
- concerns about becoming a parent
- feeling self-conscious about having sex while the baby is right there

Try talking to your partner openly about any fears he might have. See if it helps when you explain that sex is not harmful during pregnancy, and encourage him to learn more about it.

Which sex positions are the most comfortable during pregnancy?

As your pregnancy progresses, you may find that the missionary position (man on top) isn't comfortable any more. Try the following instead:

- Get on top. This keeps the weight off your tummy and lets you control the depth of penetration.
- Lie with your bottom on the edge of the bed, with your partner kneeling or standing in front of you.
- Straddle your partner while he sits in a chair. This is another position that puts no weight on your tummy.
- Try getting on your hands and knees in the doggy position.
- Lie side-by-side in the spoons position.
- Sit on a table or counter.

- Have sex standing up.

You can have satisfying sex when you're pregnant, and where there's a will, there's a way! Communication and openness are always the secret to a good sex life, and this is still true while you're pregnant.

7 Ways to Get in the Mood for Pregnancy Sex

Gone off sex now that you're pregnant? While this is perfectly normal, there are benefits to pregnancy sex. Here, experts share their tips for getting in the mood.

Feeling exhausted, queasy, and uncomfortable in your ever-changing body isn't exactly a recipe for romance. ("Not tonight, honey, I've got to throw up!") But the physical changes of pregnancy can also set the stage for amazing sex. Increased blood flow can give you a spectacular sensitivity in all your erogenous zones. "Just about everything is more sensitive – lips, vagina, clitoris, and breasts," says sex educator Lou Paget.

Plus, staying connected with your partner is more important than ever, since your baby will depend on your united front for love and stability. "Pregnant women with strong healthy relationships lead to healthier behaviors during pregnancy and better birth outcomes," explains Brett Worly, MD, an Ob-Gyn and female sexual dysfunction expert at The Ohio State University Wexner Medical Center in Columbus. New York City-based sex therapist Madeleine Castellanos, MD, adds that intimacy helps provide feelings of happiness, pleasure, closeness, and vitality.

Here's how to take advantage of everything pregnancy has to offer in the bedroom.

Take It Slow

If you're feeling anxious about pregnancy sex, don't sweat it. "Pregnancy is not a time to pressure a woman into sex, make her feel bad about her body, or make her feel guilty if her libido is not as strong as it once was," Worly says. "Increasing desire and emotional connection can be really helpful in any person and at any time, and pregnancy is no exception." He recommends studying up with books such as Rekindling Desire or Passionate Marriage. Then, try focusing on what gives pleasure, be it a foot massage (which increases oxytocin and arousal), or self-pleasuring.

Take Advantage of Your Second Trimester

During pregnancy, sex may come to a grinding halt, especially at first. "Usually women are much less amorous during their first trimester simply because they just don't feel well," says Castellanos. The good news? Many women feel better during the second trimester, so it's worth getting in as much as you can those three months, since the third trimester brings further obstacles (hello, huge bump!).

Put Matter Over Mind

Impediments to intercourse are often more than just physical. "Body parts that were usually used mostly for sexual intimacy now have implications beyond that role, as motherhood approaches," Worly explains. You may also worry (unnecessarily) that intercourse will harm the baby. "The design of a woman's body is such that a baby is well protected in the uterus during pregnancy. Because of the cervix, the penis cannot touch the baby and so cannot hurt the baby at all! Sexual activity is no more dangerous or disturbing for a fetus than the woman riding in a car over potholes or a speed bump," Castellanos reassures. "I recommend that partners focus on what is most erotic for them in order to fill their mind with sexy thoughts rather than anxious thoughts that will keep them disconnected from their own arousal."

No Screens in Bed

Ditching distracting technology from the bedroom can help boost your one-to-one time. After all, physical intimacy grows out of an emotional connection, Worly says: "Optimally couples would have 30-60 minutes daily to connect in an uninterrupted, screen-free zone."

Cultivate a Dirty Mind

Thinking about sex – even when you're not in the middle of it – will keep you in the right frame of mind when you are. "It's vital that couples create space for the erotic in their lives – both with time set aside for sex and closeness, as well as with mental attention devoted to positive thoughts about sex," Castellanos says.

Use Lube

Pregnancy hormones can cause vaginal dryness, according to Castellanos. "When couples are ready for intimacy, using a lubricant will help make things more pleasurable and erotic," she says.

Find the Right Position

Be sure to find a comfortable position for sex – and getting creative with pillows helps! "Usually laying on her left side will be the most comfortable without decreasing circulation to the baby," Castellanos advises.

How to Enjoy Sex During Pregnancy

Sex during pregnancy is perfectly safe for most women, though desire for sex may change during different stages of pregnancy — and certain adjustments may have to be made.

Among the more enjoyable changes pregnancy brings to many women is a heightened sex drive and strong orgasms during some stages of pregnancy.

For most women, intercourse during pregnancy is perfectly safe. If the pregnancy is progressing normally, sex is in no way harmful to the baby, says Annette Perez-Delboy, MD, associate clinical professor in the department of obstetrics and gynecology at Columbia University Medical Center in New York City.

Your baby is well protected within your uterus. Amniotic fluid cushions the baby, and a thick mucus plug seals the cervix tight to guard against infection, Dr. Perez-Delboy says. Although an orgasm may cause some uterine contractions, they're not labor pains, so there's no need to worry, she adds.

A pregnant woman's sex drive typically spikes in the second trimester, when energy levels rise and nausea subsides. Sex may be on your mind a lot due to an increase in blood flow to the vagina, says Perez-Delboy. The vagina becomes more engorged and vaginal lubrication increases. As a result, your desire to have sex rises and orgasms become stronger.

As your anatomy changes and you experience pregnancy weight gain, getting the most enjoyment from intercourse may call for variations to your usual routine.

Enjoying Sex During Pregnancy

You may find that this is a time of sexual freedom and, if this is your first pregnancy, you may appreciate intimacy more during you and your partner's last months without the responsibilities of parenthood. As your sexual desires peak, you may need to make some adjustments for your own comfort, depending on the stage of pregnancy you're in.

Experiment with new sexual positions. When pregnancy weight gain causes your belly to enlarge, try lying on your side during sex, either facing toward or away from your partner, suggests Perez-Delboy. Having the woman on top may also be more comfortable, because she can control the depth of penetration. Other options are for the woman to position herself on hands and knees with her partner kneeling behind or for her to sit on his lap.

Women shouldn't lie flat on their back in late pregnancy because the weight of the baby and the weight of their partner may put pressure on the inferior vena cava, a large vein that brings blood back to your heart. Pressure can cause dizziness and cause your heart rate to speed up, Perez-Delboy says.

Put safety first. If your partner has a history of sexually transmitted disease (STD) or if there's even a possibility of STD or HIV exposure when you're having sex, always use a condom. HIV can be transmitted to the baby, and some other STDs can be transmitted to the baby during delivery.

While oral sex during pregnancy is generally permissible, remember that it's never safe to blow air into the vagina because this could cause an air embolism (in which a blood vessel becomes blocked by air bubbles), which could become life-threatening. Doctors don't recommend anal sex during pregnancy because it could spread bacteria from the rectum to the vagina and possibly cause an infection, Perez-Delboy says. It also may be uncomfortable due to hemorrhoids during pregnancy.

Communicate openly. You and your partner may have different ideas about how often to have sex during pregnancy. Talk about each other's changing needs. If intercourse when pregnant becomes difficult, particularly in the final stage of pregnancy, find ways other than penetration to be close, such as using massage or cuddling.

When Sex During Pregnancy Isn't Safe

Your doctor may tell you not to have sex while pregnant if:

- You're at risk for a miscarriage.
- You're at risk for preterm labor, which is giving birth before 37 weeks.
- You have placenta previa, in which the placenta is covering the cervical opening.
- You're experiencing vaginal bleeding, which is more common when you're pregnant with twins or triplets.
- You have an infection.
- Your membranes have ruptured.
- You have a short cervix, which increases risk for miscarriage or preterm labor, or the cervix has opened.

Expect pregnancy to bring waves of changes — physical, emotional, and sexual. By listening to your body and recognizing your needs, you will be better able to enjoy the unique pleasures of this special time in your life.

The Best Sex Positions During Pregnancy

Which pregnancy sex positions are safe, and which ones are comfortable? Here's more on sex positions to try when you're pregnant.

When it comes to pregnancy sex, "Is it safe?" is probably the very first question on your mind. But after clearing that up, you might be wondering how to make the whole thing work.

Sex while you're expecting can be a little different than it was pre-pregnancy. As your tiny baby bump blossoms into a full-fledged belly, not every position might be comfortable — or satisfying — for you and your partner.

Don't worry, though. Even though having sex while pregnant might seem like unfamiliar territory, there are still plenty of pregnancy sex positions that will feel good. And you can use them up until the very end.

Here's a look at the best sex positions during pregnancy, whether there's anything you need to avoid and how to stay comfortable trimester by trimester.

What are the best pregnancy sex positions?

The good news: Almost any position works as long as you're comfortable. The not so good? As your pregnancy progresses, you might find that your ever-growing belly gets harder to maneuver around.

During your first trimester, there's a high chance that almost any sex position will feel good, assuming you feel good. Nothing kills the mood faster than early pregnancy symptoms like nausea, bloating, constipation and exhaustion. So feel free to stick with the go-tos that you and your partner liked best before finding out you were expecting.

Things can start to change once you reach your second trimester and beyond. Again, as long as a pregnancy sex position feels good, it's perfectly fine. But if it seems like your bump is getting in the way, there are plenty of belly-friendly options for you and your partner to try:

Side-lying positions: Lying on your side is often the most comfortable, whether you're facing front-to-front or front-to-back. Both options keep the weight off your back, and you won't have to worry about holding up the weight of your belly. If you feel pressure on your low back, try tucking a pillow between your knees and have your partner lie behind you.

Woman on top: The classic "cowgirl" position works because it doesn't put any pressure on your belly, and it enables you to control the depth of penetration and clitoral stimulation. One thing to keep in mind: Late in pregnancy, when your belly has gotten bigger than you ever thought possible, you could find it tough to maneuver into this position.

Rear entry: Having your partner enter you from behind means he can bypass your belly altogether. Try standing with your hands against the wall, or having your partner sit on a chair with you sitting on his lap facing away from him. Getting on all fours is another option. Just rest your arms and head on the bed so you don't have to hold up all that belly weight.

Man on top: Missionary-style is fine for a quickie, as long as your partner keeps his weight off you by supporting himself with his arms. If he prefers to have his hands free, try moving to the edge of the bed: Lie on your back on the bed, then scooch down so that your bottom is at the edge of the bed and your legs are dangling down towards the floor. Then have your partner kneel or stand in front of you. Tucking a few pillows under your back can help relieve any pressure.

What sex positions should I avoid during pregnancy?

Unless your doctor tells you otherwise, there's almost nothing that's off-limits. By the second trimester, you'll want to steer clear of any position that puts weight on your belly, like your partner lying directly on top of you or you lying on your stomach, and anything that keeps you on your back for too long.

So feel free to stick with most of the pre-pregnancy favorites that still work for you. And have fun exploring! Trying new things in the bedroom can make you and your partner feel even more connected.

Are there any risks associated with certain pregnancy sex positions?

Again, almost any position is okay as long as it feels good to you. Assuming you have the all-clear from your doctor, having sex during pregnancy is perfectly safe. That said, there are a few things to consider to avoid putting you or your baby at risk:

Keep man-on-top sessions short after week 20. Lying on your back for a few minutes isn't a big deal. But staying that way for an extended period can make you dizzy and reduce blood flow to the baby, not to mention put uncomfortable pressure on your back.

Be smart about anal sex. It's totally fine, but if you want to follow up with vaginal sex, make sure you and your partner wash up thoroughly first to keep any infection-causing bacteria at bay. Also, you'll probably want to avoid it if you're dealing with hemorrhoids — which can get uncomfortable.

What pregnancy sex positions are best by trimester?

It's all about what feels right to you. But in general, here's what you might find works best:

First trimester: Your bump is teeny-tiny to non-existent right now, so any positions that worked pre-pregnancy are probably still feeling good.

Second trimester: As you get bigger, now might be the time to start exploring positions that work around your belly. Since you aren't huge yet, you might find side-lying, rear-entry, woman-on-top and man-on-top positions comfortable.

Third trimester: It's totally fine to stick with whatever still feels okay, of course. But if some of your second-trimester favorites have started to get a little challenging, lying on your side with a pillow between your knees and having your partner enter from behind might be the most comfortable, since you won't have to support the weight of your belly or put pressure on your back.

Can I still have sex at 40 weeks and beyond?
Yes, unless your doctor has specifically told you otherwise. That said, sex at 40 weeks pregnant and beyond might come with a few surprises. For instance, you might experience slight spotting now that your cervix has started to soften. Don't worry — it's normal.

The main thing to remember: There's really no right or wrong way to have sex during pregnancy, but the bigger your belly gets, you'll very likely find that certain positions are just more comfortable. It's all about listening to your body and doing what feels right — so go for it!

Pregnancy Sex Positions That Are Absolute Fire

How does that old saying go? "Pizza is a lot like sex: When it's good, it's really good. And when it's bad… it's still pretty good." OK, that's probably true for pizza, but there's just no excuse for bad sex — even if you're pregnant.

It may take a minute to find your groove during your pregnancy, but what better time to experiment?

If you're wringing your hands about whether pregnant sex is safe, don't stress. Some couples tend to worry that intercourse could hurt or even hurry their baby right out.

Nope. Fake news. Don't let these janky old myths steal your O.

Pregnant sex is totally safe to enjoy (with the exception of high-risk pregnancy factors like placenta previa), and it's good for the momma-to-be and her partner.

As long as you're physically comfortable, almost everything is on the table. So, unless your doctor has given you the red light for some reason, you have every right to get busy.

Lucky for you, we've compiled the best positions for getting jiggy during your pregnancy. (You're welcome.)

1. Get on top

Yes, you're the Christmas tree topper, you're the shining star. In this boss move, you're in control of it all — pace, angle, etc. Meanwhile, your partner gets the full 5-star view of your beautiful self.

This one is always a go-to, but while pregnant, you may find that your body is more sensitive than usual. Being on top means you're operating the control panel and can guide yourself to an oh-so-perfect climax while also being as gentle as you need. Cheers!

2. From behind

You know the drill: You're on your hands and knees while your partner enters from behind. This one is classic and is easy to pull off while pregnant, since you have lots of grounded limbs for support so you can worry less about balance and groove.

One note: If you find this position causes back pain, use it sparingly. We've got plenty of other moves on this list if you need to switch it up!

3. Reverse cowgirl

The clitoral stimulation is off the charts here because you're the one holding the reins, cowgirl. All you do is (gently) get on top and turn around, so you're facing your partner's feet. Now your booty is facing your partner while you ride on.

Leaning forward or backward gives you the freedom to hit the spot, wherever it may be. Just hold on to your partner's legs or knees for support. Happy trails!

4. O.G. oral

No fancy maneuvering, no straining. This fan favorite doesn't need penetration to have a good time. Oral stimulation is good for all trimesters and gives you a beautiful opportunity to lay back and tune out. Get it, girl.

5. Spooning

Cue the "awww"s. Spooning is not just for, er, spooning. Lying on your side means you're nice and comfortable while your belly is out of the way.

Due to its gentle nature, this one is probably best when your belly is at its biggest. Cuddling while sexing? Not a bad BOGO.

6. Anal

Bet you thought this one wouldn't make the list. That's where you're wrong, kiddo.

There are some ground rules, though…

What you'll need:

- a good splashing of lube
- a fair amount of foreplay to get things warmed up
- a condom (to steer clear of STIs and bacteria)

Check your list and enjoy! Just be sure to take it slow and easy at first. This one is safe for all trimesters, but you'll need to proceed with caution.

Best practice for anal means no transferring of hands, toys, tongues, or penises from booty to vag. Swapping like this can be messy — literally — and can complicate your pregnancy.

7. Standing

Go ahead and lean against a wall to test this one out. Standing up is fun in the first and second trimester, but you may get a little pooped in this position when your belly grows bigger.

Just stand with your hands on the wall and spread 'em (like you're being frisked). This is a good way to get some support, and it makes for super easy access to be taken from behind. It's a good role-play opportunity too. Think police officer hat and cuffs.

8. Seated

Take a seat! This one speaks for itself, and you have a couple options.

1. While your partner sits any old where (probably on the edge of some sturdy furniture), sit facing away from

them. Now you're both comfortable and your partner's hands are free to roam. This is a good time to have your breasts or clit stroked.

2. You sit somewhere comfortable, facing your partner, and let them do their thing.

Either option delivers max satisfaction while you relax and enjoy the ride. Take a load off, sis.

9. Side by side

This one is sweet and romantic. You and your partner lie facing each other, and one of you swings your leg over the other. You're on your side (again, so comfortable), and you can keep one leg straight to get a nice angle going.

Feel free to gaze deeply into each other's eyes, since you're cheek to cheek here, while staying totally cozy in bed. Too cute.

10. Scissor

This move is as gentle as a lamb. Since your legs are intercrossed, this position makes for slower penetration, which you may appreciate during more sensitive or sore times. Still sexy, still gets the job done.

11. Tabletop

Ahhhhhhh. This one is beyond comfy. Just lie down with your booty on the edge of a bed, couch, table, whatever, and have your partner support your legs by holding them on either side of their body while standing.

They enter from this position and boom — you're both comfortable and ready for action. It's a win-win.

12. Kneeling reverse cowgirl

Ride 'em, cowgirl (again). This time, your partner is kneeling (instead of lying down) while you lean back onto them, reverse cowgirl-style. This means little pressure on your back and a nice transition move into doggy style (in case you were looking for one).

13. Edge of desire

This move has you chilling on the edge of a bed (or futon or whatever — you do you!), simply sitting up while your partner is leaning or on their knees on the floor in front of you.

They scoop you up and bring you in nice and close, and you both have at it. Another nice opportunity to sit down while living your best life.

While you're gettin' busy, stay away from these moves

There are some moves you'll want to avoid — luckily, they're the more basic (read: boring) ones.

Missionary (your partner on top). Old Reliable here can actually restrict blood flow to momma and baby. Hit the snooze button on this one until after baby arrives.

Anything flat on your tummy. For obvious reasons, lying on your stomach for any reason, sexy time or not, is not going to be super comfortable or safe while you're pregnant.

PSA: Don't blow it. While this isn't a move per se, don't let air get blown up there. When your partner is servicing you orally or otherwise, make sure they don't blow air directly into your vagina. Although it's rare, a sudden burst of air can cause an air embolism, which can be very dangerous, even fatal (whoa).

Pro tips for the best sex ever

Listen, your body is busy creating an actual human — it's cool if you're tired! You can still get it on while relaxing. Take note and take it easy, momma.

Toys

Time to crack open your toy box. Or better yet, do some sexy shopping if your current collection just won't cut it. Toys are a fun way to spice things up. Plus, they're a speedy, non-laborious way to the job done — a total bonus when you're pregnant.

Mutual masturbation

Sometimes this option just doesn't get enough love. For those times you're totally zonked but still horny as a rhino, either give each other a hand — literally — or watch each other indulge in some self-love.

Mirror, mirror on the wall...

When your belly is growing, it may be tougher to see what's going on down there. Mirrors can point you in the right direction — plus, they're hot. Your partner will have no qualms about the double vision. Helpful and sexy?

Pillow fight

Go ahead and stock up on some comfy pillows and toss them into any of these positions for more support, better angles, comfort, you name it. Create the pillow fort of your dreams and get it on.

Things You Should Know Before Having Pregnancy Sex

Your body goes through a whole host of changes when you're pregnant, and your sex drive — and sex life — aren't immune. And the differences aren't universal: While some notice increased libido, others may feel their desire drop. Whitney Port, for example, recently appeared on the podcast LadyGang to share that she just can't get into sex during pregnancy. "It is so not for me! It's not. I feel so uncomfortable with my body that I can't get into the mood," she said.

Maybe you're nodding in agreement with Port, maybe you adore pregnancy sex, and maybe you're just curious about what to expect of sex when you're expecting.

1. Body insecurity and symptoms such as fatigue and morning sickness can contribute to aversion to sex, which is not an uncommon feeling.

Dr. Ofman tells us she's heartened to see a public figure like Port open up about pregnancy body insecurities: "I think that has the potential to take some pressure off for some women who feel uneasy with their reduced interest in pregnancy, since common wisdom says that often women get more interested when they are pregnant," she says. The truth is that different trimesters are different for everyone. Dr. Van Kirk says that for some, the first trimester is the biggest mood-killer, as that's when morning sickness usually occurs. Fatigue during the first trimester is also common. "Later in the pregnancy, [a growing body] may also create a since of insecurity within the woman," she says, making it difficult to feel sexy. If you find this to be the case for you, know that you're not alone — and that it could help to voice your feelings to your partner. And on that note...

2. You may not be the only one feeling unsure about sex during your pregnancy: Your partner may be feeling it, too.

Dr. Van Kirk points out that the partner of a pregnant person "may be unsure how to initiate sex, how to find ways to position themselves, or may be afraid of hurting his pregnant partner or the gestating baby." If you feel your partner has lost interest in sex during your pregnancy, one of these concerns could be at the root of it.

3. Increased blood flow can mean higher sex drives for some pregnant people.

"Interest in sex during pregnancy waxes and wanes according to hormones, body image, and stressors," Dr.

Van Kirk says. "Some women actually notice a rise in their libido and because of increased genital blood flow and lubrication, many find they are more orgasmic." Marin agrees that sex during pregnancy can feel even better than usual — and that having sex brings benefits either way. "Your hormone levels and blood flow can increase your vaginal lubrication and your overall sensitivity," she says. "Plus, having sex releases oxytocin, a hormone known to promote relaxation, trust, and comfort." (She points out that it's also possible pregnancy may not affect your libido at all.)

4. Remember to think beyond vaginal sex.

If penetrative sex isn't appealing, Dr. Ofman says activities such as "caressing, holding, kissing, manual stimulation, oral stimulation, using a vibrator, [and] massage" are wonderful ways to connect. "Both men and women can feel awkward having vaginal intercourse during the later part of a pregnancy, and while they may feel sexually interested, they may fulfill that interest in other, non-penetrative ways," she explains. With so many different forms of intimacy on the menu, penetrative sex shouldn't be the be-all and end-all in your sex life even when you're not pregnant. And, as always, foreplay is important to get you in the mood. Dr. Van Kirk cites foot rubs and back massages as warm-ups that may be especially welcome during pregnancy.

5. Avoid sex on your back, particularly late in pregnancy.

Positions in which the pregnant person is on their back may not be very comfortable, especially during the third trimester. By that point, lying on your back can strain your hips (and also decrease the amount of blood flowing to the baby).

6. Receiver-on-top, spooning, and doggy style positions may offer the most comfort.

Dr. Ofman recommends side-by-side penetration from behind in a spooning position, as it relieves belly pressure and allows for clitoral stimulation. Marin, meanwhile, vouches for receiver-on-top (also known as cowgirl) and reverse receiver-on-top, since you "can control the depth, angle, and pace, so you can make sure you're comfortable." She also suggests a modified doggy style in which you support yourself on your elbows: "Going down on your elbows can make the penetration of normal doggy style less intense, while still letting you have some of the fun you had in your pre-pregnancy days."

7. Don't shy away from sex toys.

As at any other time, "Using sex toys [during pregnancy] can improve orgasmic response," Dr. Van Kirk says. What's more, orgasms can help you feel a sense of control over your body as you prepare to give birth. Make sure to use toys with body-safe materials such as silicone, stainless steel, or tempered glass, and completely clean them before and after use. (These materials can be washed with soap and water or even boiled as long as the toy in question doesn't contain a motor.)

8. Get wet — all over.

Dr. Van Kirk says that having sex in water can create a sensation of weightlessness that feels especially sexy and playful during pregnancy. It's also often much easier for pregnant people to get into a variety of different positions when underwater, which can be a huge turn-on.

The bottom line? Everyone experiences pregnancy differently, and there's nothing abnormal about experiencing either higher or lower libido during it. Check in often with yourself and your partner about how you're feeling so that sex can play exactly the role you want it to.

Is oral sex safe during pregnancy?

Oral sex is safe, provided that you and your partner don't have any sexually transmitted infections (STIs). Oral sex can be a great alternative if your doctor or midwife has advised you to avoid vaginal sex, for example, if you have cervical weakness or a low-lying placenta.

If either of you has an STI, you need to use protection, either a dental dam or a condom, depending on who's giving and receiving. A dental dam is a thin piece of latex that's put over your clitoris, labia and vagina.

Without protection, there's a chance that an STI, such as gonorrhoea, chlamydia and herpes, or human papilloma virus (HPV), could pass between you. Some STIs can cause pregnancy complications, and can harm your unborn baby.

It's also sensible to use protection if either of you has any cuts or sores in or on your mouth and lips.

If you're receiving oral sex while pregnant, your partner should be careful not to blow air into your vagina. It's possible for an air bubble to block one of your blood vessels. This is known as an air embolism, and it can be potentially fatal for you and your baby. It's extremely rare, but it's important to know about it, just in case.

Your partner could accidentally blow air into you if he puts his tongue inside your vagina and breathes heavily. It's probably safer if your partner sticks to kissing and licking your clitoris and the lips around your vagina (labia).

As your body changes, it's natural for you to have different needs, so keep talking to your partner and paying attention to each other's feelings.

Is anal sex safe during pregnancy?
In most cases it's safe to have anal sex, as long as you're feeling well and have no pregnancy complications.

You'll need to use plenty of lubricant. Ask your partner to be extra gentle, and listen to each other throughout. Any kind of sex can feel different when you're pregnant. If it feels uncomfortable or painful, tell him straight away so he can stop.

You should not have anal sex at all if:

- You have piles (haemorrhoids). Anal sex can make your piles bleed heavily, meaning you lose a lot of blood. This can be dangerous for you and your baby.
- You have a low-lying placenta (placenta praevia). Anal sex can damage the placenta if it covers all or part of your cervix. There's only a thin wall of tissue separating your vagina from your rectum. There's a risk that your partner's penis may push against the placenta, causing heavy vaginal bleeding.
- You have little cuts in your anus (anal fissures). Constipation is common in pregnancy and

straining to poo may result in fissures forming. These may bleed and hurt during anal sex.

- You or your partner have a sexually transmitted infection (STI). It's easier to pass on STIs through anal sex than vaginal sex.

Just as when you're not pregnant, don't switch from anal to vaginal sex without your partner first washing his genitals and changing condoms, if you're using one. Otherwise, you could be at risk of bacterial vaginosis, which has been linked with miscarriage.

My partner won't have sex with me now I'm pregnant. What can I do?

It's not unusual for men to be worried about hurting the baby when their partner is pregnant. Many men also lose their libido briefly as they cope with the changes that come with being a dad-to-be. For some men the changes to your body – like larger breasts – are wonderful. But your partner may also worry that your body somehow "belongs to the baby" right now. Don't worry, this is normally a passing phase.

The first thing to do is to sit down with your partner and find out why he's gone off sex. Just allowing him to explain what he's thinking – however strange it seems to you – will help him get through this blip.

Next, think about other ways to stay close. Pregnancy can be a great opportunity for couples to expand their sex life. Sex doesn't have to solely focus on intercourse but can include sensual touching (stroking, cuddles and massage), oral sex and mutual masturbation.

These ways of being intimate can really enhance your sex life. Not only does it provide variety, but once your baby arrives you'll have options to choose from. Even if you're too tired for intercourse, you'll still be able to find ways of being physical together.

If your partner seems to have shut down this option, there may be a conflict between what he is saying and how his body is feeling.

It's easy to reject everything beyond intercourse as not proper sex. But if your partner allows himself to be seduced by you, he could find his body has other ideas and you can both start to explore a whole new sensual world together.

If your lacklustre love life is taking its toll on your relationship in other ways, get tips on how to resolve your differences calmly.

Is it safe to masturbate or use sex toys during pregnancy?

As long as you're enjoying a healthy, low-risk pregnancy, it's perfectly safe to masturbate or use sex toys if you follow a few basic precautions.

Some women find their sex drive skyrockets during pregnancy, thanks to increased levels of the hormones oestrogen and progesterone. On top of this, the extra blood flow that pregnancy brings to the vulva and vagina can make you more responsive to touch.

However, many women find they lose interest in sex of any kind during pregnancy, and it's quite common for pregnant women to have less sex than before they conceived. This can be due to feeling tired or nauseous, or because of worries or concerns about how their body is changing.

As long as you have a healthy pregnancy the good news is that carrying on your usual sex life, with your partner, won't cause any harm at all. A healthy sex life can be an important part of keeping your relationship alive and strong. However, as your pregnancy progresses, you may want to try different things other than penetrative sex to carry on feeling satisfied and intimate.

Masturbation, either on your own or with your partner, can be particularly satisfying if your growing bump means your preferred sex positions are uncomfortable now. It needn't be any different during pregnancy than at any other time.

Similarly, if you like to use sex toys, there's no reason to stop now, although there are some precautions you should take.

Keeping your sex toys clean will protect you against most vaginal infections. That's important during pregnancy because an untreated vaginal infection may increase the risk of having your baby too early. You might not be aware if you have an infection as many people don't have any symptoms, so it's important to maintain good hygiene at all times. Here's how to keep your sex toys safe:

clean them all over (including the handle and any buttons) with warm, soapy water after every use

rinse them thoroughly and always dry them carefully before putting them away

store them in a clean, dry place

You can also reduce the risk of infection by making sure that you and your partner wash before and after sex. And it's a good idea to have a wee after using any sex toys.

Washing your toys may not be enough to remove all viruses or bacteria. Bacteria that live in your anus can cause an infection if they are transferred to your vagina, and even if you clean your sex toy thoroughly, the risk may remain. To avoid an infection don't use the same toy in your anus as you use in your vagina. Or put a new condom on your toy whenever you switch from anal to vaginal penetration.

Sharing sex toys can also be risky. The safest option is not to share, but if you are using a vibrator or strap-on and want to share it with your partner, at the very least use a new condom when you swap over.

Now that you're pregnant, you may find that using sex toys is more sexually satisfying than before. The increased blood flow to your genitals along with hormonal changes can make orgasms more intense.

Be aware that an orgasm can trigger mild cramps, known as Braxton Hicks, which will slowly fade away. These are normal and nothing to worry about unless they become regular and more painful. In this case, contact your midwife.

Foreplay can be enhanced by sex toys too. If your partner is male, and you've gone off full, penetrative sex during pregnancy, sex toys can help you maintain a loving intimacy.

When is it not safe to use a sex toy?
Your doctor or midwife may recommend that you avoid sexual activity of any kind, including anal and oral sex, masturbation and using sex toys, if:

- you have a history of cervical weakness
- you have a low-lying placenta (placenta praevia)
- you had heavy bleeding during your pregnancy
- you had a vaginal infection during your pregnancy

- you are having more than one baby
- your partner has a sexually transmitted infection

If you've experienced vaginal bleeding, talk to your midwife or GP before using sex toys, or having sex. A little bleeding after sex may be nothing to worry about, and may be caused by the cervix being irritated. But it's always best to be cautious. So tell your midwife or GP if you have any bleeding at any time.

Bear in mind that a vibrator is harder than a penis. So if your vagina feels more sensitive during pregnancy, tell your partner to be a little gentler with you.

www.ingramcontent.com/pod-product-compliance
Lightning Source LLC
Chambersburg PA
CBHW070322160726

47999CB00003B/1106